Blossoms too beautiful for words,
a spot of shade, a home for birds,
Wood for all man's needs,
and a heart that warms the seeds
of human love beneath its sheltering boughs.

Anonymous

FLOWERING TREES

Tree of Gold *(Tabebuia caraiba)*

There are over 200 species of *Tabebuia* having flowers of various colors, especially pink or yellow. Most of the *Tabebuia* trees in Florida have yellow flowers.

Many of these trees have been planted in the Sarasota area. They are very popular for street plantings in Florida communities because the beautiful blooms appear at the peak of the tourist season.

The Tree of Gold is also called Yellow Poui and Silver Trumpet Tree. The wood of some of the *Tabebuia* species is excellent for construction, but not the species grown in Florida. In parts of South America this tree is thought to be so beautiful that individual trees are sometimes dedicated to particularly favored Catholic saints.

Queen's Crape Myrtle
(Lagerstroemia speciosa)

This tree is also known as Giant Crape Myrtle, African Queen, and the Rose of India. It is not a member of the Myrtle family despite some of its common names. *Speciosa* means showy or beautiful.

Royal Poinciana *(Delonix regia)*

This may be the showiest of all Florida trees. The flaming red color really changes the landscape when these trees are in bloom. The tree canopy has a unique, wide, flat shape. It is also known as Flamboyant or Flame Tree and is native to Madagascar.

At a glance it seems that some flowers are solid red in color while the other flowers have both red and white petals. However, close inspection shows that every flower has one white petal. In some of the flowers the white petal is folded up. These flowers then appear to be solid red. The white petal may serve as a "nectar guide" for pollinators since the unfolding of the white petal seems to coincide with the ripening of the pollen.

This tree will lose its leaves and long, heavy seedpods will hang on the branches for months. The flowers appear on the bare branches but are soon joined by a growth of green foliage which adds sparkle and contrast to the incredible red blossoms.

Frangipani *(Plumeria* spp.*)*

Like many other flowers, the Frangipani blossoms of different colors have different fragrances. Frangipani is native to tropical America and the flowers are used for leis in Hawaii. In India it is planted around temples, hence the common name, Temple Tree.

During winter, the tree may briefly lose all its leaves and display an interesting pattern of bare branches. Branches of Frangipani do not taper much. Even the new twigs are unusually thick and sausage-like.

Golden-Rain Tree
(Koelreuteria elegans)

This tree blooms in the fall and is covered with bright yellow flowers. These are soon followed by the even more attractive puffed-up, papery, seedpods.

It is not unusual to see trees in bloom that have both the yellow flowers and the reddish seedpods at the same time. A photograph of such a tree appears on the back cover of this book. The Golden-Rain Tree is native to Taiwan and Fiji.

Geiger Tree (*Cordia sebestena*)

The Geiger Tree is a small tree which is native to the Florida Keys. It is salt resistant and blooms throughout the year. It has brilliant clusters of small orange flowers.

It is home to the Geiger Beetle, a small jewel-like insect that lives and feeds on the Geiger Tree only. Most Geiger Trees have them. If you look closely and turn over a few leaves, you will most likely find one.

Jacaranda (*Jacaranda mimosifolia*)

This tree has bell-shaped flowers and fern-like leaves. It is native to Brazil and quite popular in Florida.

The beautiful light-colored wood is used in carpentry. This tree has been planted in large numbers as a street tree in Johannesburg, South Africa and in Southern California.

Jacaranda is one of many trees in the world called Fern Tree as a common name. Because of its wispy foliage, Jacaranda may be the most deserving of this title.

Acacia *(Acacia spp.)* *

The more than 600 species of Acacia all have flowers which are one of two types: balls or spikes. Both kinds grow in Florida.

The flowers are sporadically fragrant. At one time they may have no noticeable scent and a little later, a wonderfully strong and pleasant perfume.

The Acacia tree is used in many rituals. A branch of Acacia is placed inside the coffin at Masonic funerals. The Shittah Tree of the Israelites was an Acacia. Its wood was used to build the Tabernacle and the Arc of the Covenant and is thought by some to have supplied Christ's crown-of-thorns.

The name Acacia derives from a Greek word meaning "thorny." In Australia where most of the Acacia species are native, the trees are called Wattles. In Africa they are simply called Thorn Trees.

*The abbreviation "spp." means "various species" and is used in this book when more than one species of a plant is grown in Florida and when it would be beyond the scope of this book to discuss all these species.

Schefflera *(Brassaia actinophylla)*

Schefflera is called the Umbrella Tree because of the shape of the leaf cluster and Octopus Tree because it has a number of bloom stalks resembling the tentacles of an octopus. Also, the flower buds resemble the suckers on an octopus tentacle.

Australian Flame Tree
(Brachychiton acerifolius)

The bark of this tree yields a fiber used in weaving baskets and other useful articles. The seeds are processed to produce a dye.

Lignum Vitae flowers

Lignum Vitae seedpods

Bottlebrush *(Callistemon* spp.*)*

Bottlebrush flowers resemble brushes used to clean laboratory bottles and test tubes. This tree is a close relative of the Punk Tree *(Melaleuca)* but does not have its aggressive tendencies to spread and crowd out other vegetation. The flowers and the seed capsules of these two trees are similar.

Lignum Vitae *(Guaiacum sanctum)*

This tree which grows in the Florida Keys produces a very dense, hard lumber which has been used for bowling balls, false teeth, and ship's propeller shafts.

It is called self-lubricating, meaning that it has sap which dries out very slowly and allows the wood to retain its resiliency. The wood of Lignum Vitae was used in making hinges for locks on the Erie Canal. These hinges remained functional for over one hundred years.

Lignum Vitae means "wood of life" and refers to the tree's medicinal value. It was the source of a once popular drug used for the treatment of syphilis.

Yellow Poinciana (*Peltophorum* spp.)

This tree is actually related to the Royal Poinciana, but not closely. Yellow Poinciana is also called Copperpod because of its beautiful maroon-colored seed-pods.

The flower sprays are useful for flower arrangements and the blooms are very fragrant. Yellow Poinciana flowers are attractive in a special way with beautiful orange-tipped stamens.

Orchid Trees

The trees in this group are not orchids at all but do have showy flowers which somewhat resemble orchids. The Latin names of all the orchid trees honor the Swiss Bauhin brothers, both of whom were famous botanists. The leaves of these trees are composed of two identical lobes which suggest the idea of brotherly closeness.

Hong Kong Orchid *(Bauhinia blakeana)*

This species of orchid tree was discovered in Hong Kong by a French priest and named for Sir Henry Blake, governor of Hong Kong in 1908. Because it never produces seeds, it is thought to be a hybrid.

Poor Man's Orchid *(Bauhinia variegata)*

This tree is different from the Hong Kong Orchid because its flower petals overlap.

White Orchid Tree
(Bauhinia variegata var. *candida)*

This is a pure-white form of the Poor Man's Orchid Tree.

Ochrosia elliptica

This tree is grown for its beautiful ornamental fruits which always appear in pairs. The fruit, although delicious looking, cannot be eaten. The leaves of this tree are actually green, not yellow like the old leaves shown in the photo.

Coral Tree (Erythrina variegata)

This exciting tree is also called Indian Tiger's Claw because each flower has one petal which is considerably longer than the others and has a sharp point.

The flowers of the Coral Tree are well designed for pollination by birds. Both the flower and its support are strong enough to hold a bird's weight, and the location of the nectar is designed for the convenience of a bird's beak.

The flowers have no fragrance, but rely on their intense color to attract pollinators. In Java the Coral Trees bloom during the dry months and their flowers are important sources of moisture for birds.

Jerusalem Thorn *(Parkinsonia aculeata)*

Jerusalem Thorn is a tropical American tree despite its common name. It has very interesting leaves which look like needles. They are not true needles like those of pine trees, but have tiny leaflets and thorns.

The Jerusalem Thorn is a rather transparent tree because the leaflets, which are small to begin with, drop in winter. There is never much up there to block the view of the sky. Nurserymen have tried to market the tree with the idea that it could screen a picture window without blocking the view from the inside.

This tree has no connection to Jerusalem but the common name may come from a belief that the tree supplied Christ's crown-of-thorns. According to another story, an old preacherman accidentally grabbed hold of the thorny branches and, after looking around to make sure that nobody nearby could hear him, hollered "Jeeee-ru-salem."

Mimosa *(Albizia julibrissin)*

Native to Iran, this tree is cold-hardy and is grown as far north as Maryland.

Pitch Apple *(Clusia rosea)*

This tree is a graffiti artist's dream. Cuts on the leaves may remain visible for more than a year. It is said that these trees were sometimes planted by the front door of a house so that visitors could sign their names, hence the title, Autograph Tree.

The Pitch Apple has a very beautiful and unusual flower. The green, wet-looking circle at the center is called a staminoidal ring and produces a sweet, sticky nectar.

The Pitch Apple, in its natural habitat, usually begins life by growing on another tree, much like the Strangler Fig. It is native to the Florida Keys and Caribbean basin.

Chinaberry (*Melia azedarach*)

Most parts of this tree, including the fruit, are dangerously narcotic if taken internally, although the fruit is enjoyed in complete safety by birds.

The poisonous fruits are used to make insect repellent and flea powder. Chinaberry fruits are packed around flowers to keep insects away. Chinaberry leaves are placed in books to keep insects from chewing on the paper or bindings and can protect stored fabrics from attack by moths.

This tree is an example of how some plants are perceived very differently in various parts of the world. Chinaberry is regarded as sacred in Ceylon where garlands of the flowers are placed on temple altars, but considered a weed and a pest in Cuba where it has overgrown many areas.

The pits of the berries are strung for rosary beads in southern Europe. The natural opening in the pit is easily enlarged with a needle. For this reason Chinaberry is also called the Bead Tree in some countries.

African Tulip Tree
(Spathodea campanulata)

Each blossom of this beautiful tree is out-lined with a thin ring of yellow color, adding punch to the already vibrant orange. The center of the flower cluster is a circle of tightly packed buds which resembles a hand of bananas. A few new buds open periodically at the outside of the circle. As they fade and die, new buds open, maintaining the perfect ring shape for a long blooming period.

Because the flower buds sometimes contain water, it has been called the Fountain Tree. Children enjoy squeezing the buds and watching them squirt water.

Woman's Tongue Tree (Albizia lebbeck)

This tree is well known for producing an abundance of long, brittle pods containing small seeds which, when driven by a light breeze, rattle endlessly. What connection this might have with a woman's tongue is not clear.

Woman's Tongue Tree is also called East Indian Walnut because of its dense, dark-brown, close-grained heartwood.

Shower Trees

There are many different shower trees growing in tropical areas of the world, each producing an abundance of blossoms. It would be hard to judge which is the most beautiful because each has its own unique style and color combinations.

Pink and White Shower
(Cassia javanica)

The flowers of this tree grow on short stems close to the branches and appear to completely wrap the branches with dense clusters of blooms.

The pink color of the blooms gradually fades so that the clusters appear to be of mixed colors. Adding to the effect are the red-colored flower stems.

Another common name for this tree is Apple Blossom Cassia. "Cassia" is an ancient word for cinnamon. The Shower Trees are not related to the cinnamon spice trees, but the connection may have resulted from native custom in using the word "cassia" to refer to various trees with useful bark.

Rainbow Shower
(Cassia fistula x Cassia javanica)

This tree is a cross between the Golden Shower and the Pink and White Shower. It has puffy flowers of intense color. No two trees are exactly the same color.

Golden Shower *(Cassia fistula)*

This native of India is one of the most ornamental of the 400 Cassia species.

It is called the Pudding Pipe Tree in India because the long, tubular seed pods contain a gelatin-like substance which holds the seeds separate in the pod.

This substance is eaten by the very poor when other food is not available, but is not recommended as food under normal conditions because it is very laxative. In some countries this substance is actually used medicinally as a laxative.

Kapok and the Bombax Trees

Many of the trees of the Bombax family have large trunks covered with sharp spines. The trunks are swollen at their bases and supported with huge buttressed roots. They grow very large in their native countries.

The seed pods are filled with a fluffy cotton fiber which is used for stuffing. Kapok fiber has five times the buoyancy of cork and is used in life jackets, sleeping bags, and mattresses.

Shaving Brush Tree
(Pseudobombax ellipticum)

The flowers emerge from pods which open at night with an audible "pop". The long buds are composed of five brown petals which curl up as the bud opens. The Shaving Brush Tree is native to Central America.

Floss Silk Tree (Chorisia speciosa)

The photograph of this tree is on the front cover. It was taken in the beautiful landscaped gardens surrounding the Miami International Airport.

An amazing fact about this South American tree is that the flowers vary considerably in shape and color from one tree to another. Neighbors have been known to argue about which one of their trees was a true Floss Silk when in fact they both belonged to this same species.

Red Silk Cotton Tree (Bombax ceiba)

The beautiful red flowers of this Asian tree attract birds and insects with sweet nectar. The flowers are eaten by small animals after they fall to the ground.

The famous tree of the Kapok Tree Inn at Clearwater is actually a Red Silk Cotton Tree just like this one. "Kapok" refers to the silky fibers found in the seed pods of several trees of the Bombax group. It also refers to a particular tree of this group, Ceiba pentandra, the so-called "true" Kapok Tree, which grows in South America and is not common in Florida. For this reason it is not quite accurate to refer to the Bombax trees of Florida as Kapok, but the name is frequently used in this way.

Male Flower

Female Flower

Fruit on Male Tree

Fruit on Female Tree

Papaya *(Carica papaya)*

The Papaya tree has a very complex reproductive system. There are trees with male flowers, trees with female flowers, trees with both kinds of flowers, and trees that change from one sex to the other.

When the fruit is borne on female trees, it forms large clusters with dozens of fruits all around the trunk. Fruit can form on the long male flower stalks too. This unusual process is called "parthenocarpy" or the production of fruit without pollination. Such fruit is usually smaller and contains no seeds. It is, however, just as delicious.

Papaya fruit is not only delicious but contains papain, an enzyme which is used by people with digestive problems.

Papaya is called Pawpaw by the British, and Fruta Bomba in Cuba where the word Papaya is an obscenity.

The photo at the top of this page shows the lavish shower of flowers which forms on the male trees. These small flowers may be either white or yellow. A photograph of a female tree appears on the back cover.

Magnolia *(Magnolia grandiflora)*

This large tree is common from Central Florida northward. The Magnolia blossom is a popular symbol of the deep South and is common in literature as part of the aura of plantation life.

These photos show the life cycle of a Magnolia flower. (1) The bud forms and opens to reveal the flower at the peak of its glory. In the Magnolia, the blossoms close a bit at night, possibly trapping beetles near the ripe pollen. (5) As the bloom fades, the petals become a garbage can for the fallen flower parts. (6) The petals wither and die. (7) The ovaries of the pollinated flower expand to form the fruit. (8) The fruit ripens to a beautiful red color. (9) Finally, the plump ripe fruit bursts open to release the seeds.

Silk Oak *(Grevillea robusta)*

The Silk Oak from Australia is not an oak tree but is called that because its woodgrain is similar to oak. This beautiful wood is used in making furniture and paneling. The flowers form an interesting brush shape.

Sausage Tree *(Kigelia africana)*

This amazing tree produces a sausage-shaped fruit which is woody and inedible but very interesting as a garden novelty. The long sausages are produced by flowers that have been cross-pollinated and the short sausages from self-pollinated flowers.

The abundant blossoms are even more fascinating. They are strictly night-blooming and open as soon as it is fully dark. By midnight or so, they have fallen to the ground, having completed their reproductive functions. The blossom cluster resembles a chandelier. Only a portion of the buds open on any one night.

The cluster hangs from a stem which may be a few feet long or as long as 25 feet. In its native Africa, the flowers are pollinated by bats. It is theorized that the long flower stems help the bats by keeping the flowers away from the thick leaves of the canopy which might confuse the bats' sonar. In Florida, these trees are usually pollinated by insects rather than bats.

Royal Palm *(Roystonea regia)*

The Royal Palm is a good candidate for the most beautiful palm in the world. At one time, these trees were common as far north as Tampa, but they are sensitive to freezes and few now exist above Sarasota with many in that area showing freeze damage.

There are two types of Royals in Florida: the Cuban Royal (*Roystonea regia*) and the native Florida Royal (*Roystonea elata*). They are very similar and difficult to distinguish without studying the seeds and the leaflets. The Cuban Royal is more common.

When a Royal Palm is not growing in nature, but has been planted by man as part of landscaping, it is probably the Cuban Royal. Some Florida native Royals can be seen growing wild at Fakahatchee Strand in the Big Cypress Preserve.

The circular bands around the trunk are scars where old fronds have been attached and then fallen off. Also, most trunks of Royal Palms host a rich variety of colorful lichens as shown in the small photo, above.

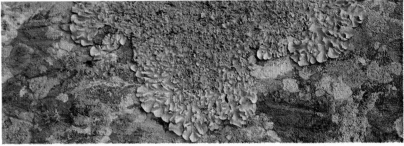

Palms around the World

There are thousands of species of palms in the world and many of them can be grown in Florida. This book illustrates only those palms that are most commonly seen around the state.

Next to grasses, palms are the most important plants in the world for human survival. They provide a major source of food, shelter, and clothing for millions of people throughout the tropics.

There are two types of palms. Fan palms have leaflets that spread out like the fingers of a hand. Feather palms have leaflets that are arranged in rows along a stem in the same manner as a feather. Scientifically, these two types are called palmate (like the fingers from the palm of a hand) and pinnate.

Coconut Palm (*Cocos nucifera*)

Years ago, the most important type of Coconut Palm in Florida was the Jamaica Tall, but a tree disease called "lethal yellowing" destroyed most of these trees in a number of areas of South Florida starting in the late 1960's. They have been replaced by several new varieties of which the Malayan Dwarf is the most commonly seen. Lethal yellowing is also a threat to many other palm species.

The coconut is one of the largest plant seeds in the world. The meat of the coconut (called "copra" in its dried form) is converted to cooking oil, margarine, and soap. The milk derived from the meat is important in many cultures for cooking. A multitude of products are produced from "coir," the husk of the coconut, including rope, brushes, and mattresses.

The word *Cocos* may have come from a Portuguese word for monkey. After the husk has been removed, the coconut has three black dots and bears some resemblance to the face of a monkey. Another possible origin is the French word "coque" meaning "shell."

Growing Low

Growing Tall

Saw Palmetto *(Serenoa repens)*

These palms grow in low clumps and clusters. The stems have small spines or teeth which are saw-like as the common name suggests.

Saw Palmetto covers a very large part of the state in a type of terrain called "pine flatwoods." Along with the pines, Saw Palmettos have the ability to withstand frequent brush fires and rejuvenate in a few months time.

You take the high road, I'll take the low road

Sometimes this palm grows very low with the trunk actually resting on the ground. Under different conditions, it can grow upright like other palms and reach heights of ten feet or more. There is speculation that the upright growth pattern occurs when the palm is in shade and must reach for the light, or when the ground is subject to standing water, but it is not hard to find the two different forms growing side by side.

While most Saw Palmettos have light-green leaves, there is a variety growing around the Atlantic coast whose leaves have a distinctively bluish color (see photo at left).

Manila Palm *(Veitchia merrillii)*

This palm is sometimes called the Little Royal because of its resemblance to the much larger Royal Palm. It is also called the Christmas Palm because of its beautiful display of red fruit which appears at the Christmas season.

Its attractive, small white flowers may be seen blooming in spring and summer. Manila Palms display either fruit or flowers almost every month of the year.

Lady Palm (*Rhapis excelsa*)

These delicate, tiny trees grow in clusters and usually do not get much taller than ten feet. The trunks are very, very slender and are covered with a matting of fiber.

The Lady Palm can prosper in the shade and is frequently used in landscaping to provide masses of foliage.

Lady Palms have been cultivated as potted plants by the Japanese for hundreds of years. Some dwarf varieties sell for thousands of dollars and are purchased as investments.

Jelly Palm (*Butia capitata*)

This tree is distinguished by the grey-green or bluish color of its leaves and also the spiral pattern of old leaf bases on its trunk.

It is very resistant to cold weather. Other than the Cabbage Palm and Saw Palmetto, it is the only palm commonly seen in the northern parts of Florida. It can grow as far north as Washington, D.C.

The fruit is used to make jelly in its native South America. Another common name is Pindo Palm.

Cocos Plumosa, Queen Palm
(Arecastrum romanzoffianum)

This palm used to be classified in the Coconut genus, hence the common name "Cocos." It was reclassified in the 1940's, but the old scientific name has remained as the most popular common name.

This palm is especially appreciated by some for its spectacular sprays of flowers and fruits which form throughout the year. Others hire tree surgeons to remove the flowers and seeds because they think they are messy.

The flower clusters burst from large pods, a feature which is common to many other palms. When the soft flesh of the fruit is removed there is a single, hard seed with three spots, like a miniature coconut. This seed is called the "monkeynut" in Hawaii and is used to make necklaces.

The scientific name of this palm will soon be changed from *Arecastrum* to *Syagrus*. Frequently, the opinions of experts differ about classification. Since there is no binding authority, plants often have various scientific names, each with its own proponents.

Cabbage Palm *(Sabal palmetto)*

This palm is a native of Florida and is also the Florida state tree. Cabbage Palms vary in appearance depending upon whether all the bases of the old leaves remain on the tree. These leaf bases, called "boots," form a criss-cross pattern on the trunk.

No one is completely sure why the boots fall off more readily from some Cabbage Palms than others. It is common to see two trees growing right next to each other, one with boots and the other with a bare trunk. When nurserymen plant this palm, they frequently remove the boots with a chain saw.

Eating Swamp-Cabbage

The leaf-producing bud of this palm is harvested as an edible delicacy. The taste of the bud is a little like raw cabbage, hence the common name of the tree, Cabbage Palm.

In the early days of Florida, picnickers could go to the riverside with a fishing pole, a frying pan, and an axe. Lunch would be freshly cooked fish and swamp-cabbage salad. This series of photos shows how the swamp-cabbage (or hearts-of-palm) is collected.

Fresh hearts-of-palm has become hard to find in present day Florida. Cabbage Palms are not as plentiful as they once were and removal of the bud kills the tree. The canned variety that is sold in groceries and some restaurants is usually imported from South America.

The photo at right shows the distinctive Cabbage Palm leaf which is partly folded in half along its curved midrib.

Washingtonia *(Washingtonia robusta)*

Because of its impressive height, this palm has been used throughout Florida to line city streets. A native of Mexico, it is also used extensively in California. It has been called the Petticoat Palm, because if it is not pruned, the dead leaves usually remain on the trunk for years until blown off by powerful storms.

The flowers form on large, drooping stalks and are followed by heavy clusters of black seeds. In Australia, this tall tree is called the Skyduster. The scientific name honors our first president, George Washington.

Cabbage Palm vs Washingtonia

When these palms are small, they have a superficial resemblance. An easy way to tell the difference is that the Washingtonia has a flat, fan-shaped leaf, but the leaf of a Cabbage Palm is folded in two down the middle. Another difference is that the stems of the Washingtonia have small, sharp thorns but the stems of the Cabbage Palm are smooth.

Fishtail Palm *(Caryota mitis)*

The Fishtail Palm, in addition to the unique shape of its leaves, has another interesting feature. Fruit is borne in many clusters starting at the top of each stalk.

As each cluster dies, another appears directly below it until the last cluster has fruited at the bottom of the stalk. At that point the entire stalk dies, but other suckers grow up to take its place.

The seeds are edible, but the pulp contains stinging crystals that can cause a severe skin rash if the fruit is not handled properly.

Another species of Fishtail Palm, *Caryota urens* is known as the Wine Palm, or Toddy Palm, because sap collected from the flower stems is used to make sugar, wine, and gin. A single tree can be tapped for as much as 12 gallons of sap. The sap of a number of other palms is also used to make sugar in many tropical regions of the world.

Paurotis Palm *(Acoelorrhaphe wrightii)*

These cluster palms are commonly seen growing wild in the wet areas of the Everglades, but they will also prosper in dry places and have been used extensively in commercial landscaping in recent years. The trunk is covered with a matting of woven fiber.

Bottle Palm *(Hyophorbe lagenicaulis)*

This palm has peculiar thickening at the bottom of its trunk resulting in its ornamental bottle shape. It is a small tree, seldom growing taller than 15 feet.

The fronds have a unique spiral twist that adds to the palm's decorative appeal. The Bottle Palm is native to the Mascarene Islands which are located near Madagascar in the Indian Ocean.

Chinese Fan Palm *(Livistona chinensis)*

This palm, which is native to China, is a graceful tree with wide fronds and leaflets that have a characteristic droop at their tips.

Solitaire Palm *(Ptychosperma elegans)*

This tree is easily recognized because the trunk is very, very slender. The fronds are also distinctive with each leaflet rather wide in the center. The brilliant red fruit can be a skin irritant for some people.

Areca Palm *(Chrysalidocarpus lutescens)*

This cluster palm from Madagascar has beautiful ringed trunks. It was once thought to be related to the true Areca Palm, a species in Asia which produces the Betel Nut. Another common name which may be more accurate is Yellow Butterfly Palm.

Thatch Palm *(Thrinax radiata)*

This palm is most frequently seen in the Florida keys. It is distinguished by its heavy, thick-looking leaves and white fruits.

The leaves have been used for the roofing of shelters, the trunks for pilings, and to build the "kraals" or enclosures, which were once common in the Keys for breeding turtles.

Date Palms *(Phoenix* spp.*)*

A number of date palms grow well in Florida, but they do not usually produce much edible fruit because there is too much rain. In drier regions, such as the Middle East, these trees are critically important as a source of food.

All date palms have leaflets which are modified into spines near the trunk of the tree. Many other palms have thorns on their leaf stems, but they are not modified leaflets.

Senegal Date *(Phoenix reclinata)*

This is a cluster palm which commonly has 8 to 15 trunks. If not trimmed, it becomes an impenetrable mass of fronds, but with pruning, the beautiful cluster shape appears.

Since date palms all bloom at about the same time, there is considerable cross-breeding, and many date palm specimens, especially the Senegal Date Palms, may be hybrids. The resulting wide variations in appearance make accurate identification of many Florida date palms very difficult, and in some cases, impossible (note the three Senegal Data Palms at left).

Pygmy Date

Pygmy Date Flowers

Pygmy Date *(Phoenix roebelenii)*

This Palm rarely exceeds ten feet in height and is attractive because of its delicate leaves and interesting trunk. It is a native of Laos and was first brought to the West by a German botanist named Roebelin who had encountered the palm in Thailand.

India Date *(Phoenix sylvestris)*

This palm resembles the Canary Island Date Palm, except that the trunk is thinner and the palm is usually taller. Like the Canary Island Date Palm, fruit appears in clusters on long, orange colored stems, but only on the female trees.

Many India Date Palms have large masses of exposed roots at their bases which may extend as high as six feet above the ground. Many palms have the potential to produce such roots, depending upon the conditions, but such roots are larger and more common with this particular species.

This type of root is technically called an "adventitious root." Like underground roots, these special roots collect water and provide support through added girth.

Canary Island Date
(Phoenix canariensis)

This palm is called the Pineapple Palm because the shape resembles a Pineapple when the palm is small. As it becomes larger, it is easily recognized as different from the other date palms because of its extremely thick, dark-colored trunk.

It is common for a variety of ferns to grow on the trunks of these palms, adding considerably to their beauty. They are, as their name implies, native to the Canary Islands which are located off the coast of northwest Africa near Morocco.

A Fashion Model's Diet

Palms are frequently pruned by people who believe that it improves their appearance. Unfortunately, much live foliage is often trimmed off along with the dead leaves to give the tree a "sharp" look. This deprives the palm of its source of nutrition and starves it.

King Sago
Female Tree

Ripe
Fruit

Detail:
New Growth

Sago Palm *(Cycas* spp.*)*

Sago Palms are not palms, but Cycads, one of the oldest plant groups. They rarely grow taller than ten feet and are seen in many home gardens throughout south Florida. Cycads have been called the "living fossils" because the Cycads growing today resemble so closely those seen in fossils from the early ages of life on earth.

Sagos Palms are either male or female. The male tree produces a cone which is slender and long. When it is ripe, it is covered with large amounts of pollen. The female trees have seeds that are formed on specialized leaves loosely arranged at the top of the trunk. After pollination, the seeds ripen to a bright red color and enlarge to the size of golf balls. The ripe fruit is covered with a powdery substance which helps retain moisture.

In a few rare cases, Sago Palms have changed sex after great injury. That is, after freezing or chopping, a tree of one sex produced the cone of the opposite sex.

Queen Sago
Female Tree

Queen Sago
Male Tree

King Sago *(Cycas revoluta)*

The King Sago is popular for bansai trees in Japan where it is native. The leaves are very stiff and sharp pointed. They almost feel like they have been cut from a piece of sheet metal with tin-snips.

The photo at right shows the cone of the male King Sago; at the top of the opposite page is the female tree; at the bottom of the opposite page are photos of new growth and a ripened seed.

Queen Sago *(Cycas circinalis)*

This Sago is sometimes called the Fern Palm although it is neither fern nor palm, but a cycad native to the Old World tropics ("Old World" refers to the eastern hemisphere).

The photo at the top of this page is the female Queen Sago. The photo below it is the male tree showing the orange-colored reproductive cone.

King Sago
Male Tree

Traveller's Palm
(Ravenala madagascariensis)

This palm-like tree, a distant relative of the Banana, is so named because the base of each leaf stem holds about a quart of fresh water which could be tapped by a thirsty traveller. There is a notion that when this plant grows in the wild, it will align itself in an East-West direction. This "living compass" idea is not true, but the seed pods are edible and a shelter from sun and rain can be constructed from the large leaves.

The shape of the Traveller's Palm resembles a folding fan, with all the leaves in one plane. These leaves are among the world's largest. A common feature is that the leaves are torn by the wind.

Ponytail Palm *(Beaucarnea recurvata)*

The greatly swollen base is a water storage area, useful in dry climates like that of its native Mexico. This strange plant is a tree member of the Lily Family. It is also called the Elephant Foot Tree. The photo at near left shows this tree in full bloom.

Screw Pine *(Pandanus spp.)*

Screw Pines have been called Walking Fences because of their abundant prop roots. When a tree is blown over by strong winds, more prop roots will form to hold the tree off the ground and it will continue growing, giving the appearance of "walking."

The leaves grow in a spiral pattern around the trunk, inspiring the common name Screw Pine. The leaves are economically useful in some tropical areas for weaving. However, the leaves must first be prepared by removing the spiny edges and the midrib, and then pounding to soften the remaining leaf fibers.

The beautiful long bloom (above) is growing from a male tree. The female trees bear a fruit which looks a little like a pineapple, but in some species ripens to a bright red color (the frog sitting on the ripe fruit is a Cuban Tree Frog). The fruit is edible but so unappealing that it is called "famine food." In Hawaii, this fruit is mockingly called the "tourist pineapple" because some first-time visitors confuse it with the real pineapples.

Red Maple *(Acer rubrum)*

This is one of the few south Florida trees which has showy fall colors and hence, when its leaves change to bright red, it really stands out from the green landscape. The fruits grow into the familiar butterfly form. This tree ranges from Florida to Nova Scotia.

Ear Tree *(Enterolobium cyclocarpum)*

These trees can have trunks 10 feet in diameter. Their curious seed pods are used as cattle feed in some countries (photo of the seed pod, upper left).

Eucalyptus *(Eucalyptus spp.)*

This tree is the source of the aromatic Eucalyptus oil which is used in inhalents and lozenges. If you crush one of the leaves, you can smell the familiar oil (bottom right).

Arborvitae *(Platycladus orientalis)*

This plant is popular with many home gardeners because it lends itself to planting in neat, tidy rows. It is also used extensively in cemetery landscaping (bottom left).

Japanese Yew *(Podocarpus macrophyllus)*

The colorful growths on this Podocarpus are a combination of seeds and arils. An aril is an appendage to the seed which may attract a variety of seed-dispersing creatures with its added food value.

Norfolk Island Pine
(Araucaria heterophylla)

This tree is native to Norfolk Island, which is off the east coast of Australia. It was discovered there by the famous explorer and adventurer, Captain Cook.

It can grow to be very tall, up to 200 feet, so it was much used for masts of sailing ships and is now popular in landscaping because of its beautiful symmetry and interesting foliage.

It has no needles and hence is not a true pine despite its common name. Instead it has tiny and densely overlapping, scale-like leaves.

Another interesting feature is the way the branches emerge from the trunk in layers with no branches between the layers. This gives the tree a unique appearance which inspired the name Pagoda Tree.

CYPRESS

Cypress in the Winter

Bald Cypress

Pond Cypress

Air Plant

Bald Cypress *(Taxodium distichum)*

Cypress trees are deciduous, losing their leaves in the winter, hence the name Bald Cypress. This gives cypress seasonal color changes and a very different appearance at different times of the year.

Cypress is generally considered to be a resident of the swamp, but cypress will also grow well in dry soil. It is seldom found in dry locations because it has thin bark and is not fire resistant like the pines. Frequent Florida brushfires kill the baby cypress everywhere except the areas which are continually wet.

Cypress may look quite different in various areas depending upon soil conditions. In some places there is a type called Pond Cypress *(Taxodium ascendens)* which has leaves tightly folded against the twigs rather than the open, feathery leaves of Bald Cypress (see photos at left: photo with cones is Pond Cypress; the photo above it, Bald Cypress). In the Everglades there is also a stunted type called Dwarf Cypress. Some experts feel that all the various types are merely varieties of a single species.

Cypress in the Summer

The function of cypress "knees" is not fully understood. Knees are extensions of the cypress roots and may reach ten feet in height. One function may be to provide the root system with oxygen. Trees growing in soil that is not water-logged usually do not develop knees. The knees may also aid in the support of the tree. In Florida the knees are harvested to produce many woodcraft products such as table-lamp bases.

Cypress Knees

In Florida, cypress is frequently seen growing in low areas called cypress "heads." A common characteristic of these clusters is the formation of a "cypress dome," a grouping of trees which is dome-shaped in appearance. The reason "cypress domes" form may be the growth process. The grouping may have started with the trees in the middle and spread outward. The trees in the center of the dome would then be the oldest. Another possibility is that the center is the wettest area giving the trees growing there an advantage during the dry season. Or, it could be that the depth of superior soil is greater at the center.

Cypress Dome

Red Mangrove

A Very Valuable Resource

Mangroves trees are extremely important to Florida. The heavy growth of mangroves along the sheltered coastlines breaks the waves of storms and prevents erosion. The roots provide protection in shallow waters which is critical for reproduction of many fish and other sea creatures essential to the food chain in the ocean. Organic debris, such as leaves falling from the trees, provides food for small marine organisms such as crabs and shrimp which in turn feed larger predators. Much of the marine life around Florida is dependent on this food chain. For this reason, the destruction of mangroves through development is a very serious problem.

There are three kinds of mangrove common in Florida. Oddly, they belong to different plant families and are not closely related. They tend to grow in different positions in relation to the water line. Red Mangrove grows right out into the bays. Black Mangrove is less tolerant of living in salt water, so it usually grows along the edge of the water. White Mangrove is generally found above the tideline. These preferences are not strictly observed, and often all three kinds of Mangrove can be seen growing together.

Red Mangrove (Rhizophora mangle)

Red Mangrove is sometimes called the Walking Tree because its roots advance out into the water a step at a time. It is the only one of the three Mangroves in Florida which has these aerial roots.

Red Mangrove has an interesting form of reproduction. It produces a long, fully germinated seedling without roots, called a "propagule" which is actually a complete plant. The propagule is ready to take root after dropping off the parent and floating to a new location.

White Mangrove
(Laguncularia racemosa)

The White Mangrove may also produce some pneumatophores, like the Black Mangrove, but they are not nearly so numerous.

Unlike Red Mangrove and Black Mangrove which reproduce by forming propagules, White Mangrove reproduces through seeds.

Red Mangrove Seedlings

Roots of Black Mangrove

Black Mangrove *(Avicennia germinans)*

Black Mangrove is the most cold resistant of the three species by at least several degrees. For this reason, Black Mangrove trees are frequently much larger than Red or White Mangroves growing in the same location. Beekeepers set out hives among these trees in early summer because the abundant flowers produce good honey.

The Black Mangrove tree produces fully germinated seedlings like the Red Mangrove, but they are very different in shape (photo, bottom left).

Black Mangrove does not have aerial support roots like Red Mangrove. Like its name implies, it does have a rather black trunk. Its most amazing feature is its unique, pencil-like roots called "pneumatophores" which grow upward as vertical extensions of underground roots. They have a fascinating appearance because they stick out of the soil in large numbers. They provide oxygen to the mangrove root system and may also provide extra support for the plant in the soft, wet soil (photo, top right).

Red Mangrove Flowers

Black Mangrove Seedling

White Mangrove Fruits

51

FICUS, FLORIDA'S SPRAWLING FIG TREES

Aerial Roots of the Weeping Banyan

Drip Tip Leaves

Bo Tree *(Ficus religiosa)*

Certain Banyans are held in high regard in India because Gautama Buddha is said to have received his enlightenment while seated under a Banyan. This particular Banyan is called the Bo Tree or Bodh Tree.

The Bo Tree is interesting because its leaves have a long slender tip called a "drip tip" which helps the leaf shed water quickly. This can help a leaf to quickly resume food production after a heavy rain. Where rains are frequent, this can be a significant advantage.

Figs are frequently mentioned in the Christian Bible and to "sit under your own vine and your own fig tree" was a common expression for peace and prosperity in Biblical times (I Kings 4:25). In parts of Africa it is believed that the spirits of the dead reside in the thick leaves of the Banyans, thus large trees are not cut down.

Weeping Banyan *(Ficus benjamina)*

This is one of the most common Banyans in South Florida. (see photo above)

"Banyan" is a common name for all Fig trees which produce multiple trunks. The word "Banyan" means "trader" or "merchant" in India where these trees are native. The traders were usually found in open air markets held under the shelter of these mammoth trees. A really large Banyan can cover several acres of land.

The auxilliary trunks start as vine-like aerial roots hanging from the branches (see photo above). Under certain conditions some of the aerial roots may wrap themselves tightly around the main trunk of the tree (photo, opposite page). When aerial roots reach the soil, they thicken and become auxilliary trunks which support enormously long branches (photo, top right, opposite page).

Auxilliary Roots

The fruits of Fig trees are actually flower clusters turned inside out so that the male and female parts are completely enclosed within the fruit as the cross section below reveals. Such a structure is known as a "syconium."

Pollination occurs when a tiny wasp (less than one mm. in size) lays eggs inside the fig (after crawling through the small opening or pore which is visible at the bottom of every fig). When the eggs hatch, the new male and female wasps mate. The males die without ever leaving the fig. The females leave the fig carrying pollen and repeat the cycle by laying eggs inside other figs and pollinating their flowers in the process.

There is a specific kind of wasp which pollinates each species of fig. Since many of these trees are not native to Florida, the wasp species necessary for pollination may not exist here. In this case, the tree will continue to produce fruit, but since the flowers are not pollinated, there will be no seeds. The species of figs grown for food are self-pollinating and do not provide homes for wasps.

Aerial Roots Wrapping Trunk

Flower Inside Fruit

Strangler Fig (*Ficus aurea*)

This is one of the most curious and interesting Florida trees. It will, after a long period of time, kill its host by covering it with too much shade, by tangling its aerial roots in the leaf bud of the host tree, or by encircling the trunk of the host and preventing it from expanding. It has been called a "vegetable octopus." This strangling process may take decades before a large host tree is subdued.

A very natural question would be, "Why does the Strangler Fig strangle? What gives it such murderous tendencies?" The process starts when a Strangler Fig seed is transported to the upper portions of a host tree by birds. The host is often a Cabbage Palm because this palm has a fibrous, criss-cross pattern of old leaf bases around its trunk which provides good rooting material for the seedling. Aerial roots are sent downward eventually reaching the ground, and new branches are sent upward. Using the tree for support, the Strangler Fig gradually establishes itself and kills its host, not out of malice, but only as a result of its own normal growth pattern.

Starting life in the branches of another tree provides a Strangler Fig with more light, an advantage over trees which start on the ground. Strangler Figs will grow if planted directly in the ground, but strangely, will not grow tall. Under these conditions they seem to lose the power to form a large trunk. The reason is not known.

Rubber Tree (*Ficus elastica*)

This tree is not related to the trees grown commercially for rubber in Asia and is quite different in appearance. Here in Florida it is grown as an ornamental, but it is a minor source of rubber in other parts of the world.

This species has been used as a popular house plant for more than 150 years. It was once so popular in Germany that it was called the Berlin Weed. In the wild it sends out aerial roots and can become very large. It also produces surface roots which undulate in all directions like snakes. For this reason it has been called the Snake Tree.

Each new leaf is housed in a colorful protective sheath which breaks open to allow the leaf to unfurl.

One feature common to all the Ficus group of trees is the abundant milky latex (sap). It can be seen to flow freely merely by snapping off a leaf.

CONTROVERSIAL TREES

Punk Tree *(Melaleuca quinquinervia)*

The Punk Tree is sometimes called the Cajeput Tree, after the name of the medicinal oil derived from its leaves. It is native to Australia and New Guinea and was imported to Florida as a very fast growing shade tree for new housing developments. It can grow in very wet areas as well as dry soil. For this reason it was seeded in the area of the Everglades in the 1930's when it was fashionable to want to dry up the swampy areas of the state. Since then it has taken over vast territory.

Punk Trees are very fire resistant. When fires destroy everything around them, Punk Trees use these periods to multiply and take over larger areas. Punk Trees produce seedlings so tightly packed together that a raccoon would have trouble getting through. When the tree is stressed by fire or when it is cut down, it immediately releases all the seeds which have been stored on its branches, waiting for the proper moment. With these tactics and no effective natural restraints, the Punk Tree has become a big problem by crowding out other vegetation over large areas.

Recently, commercial ventures to process Punk Trees for wood chips have started operation. Efforts have been under way for years now to find uses for the excess Punk Trees.

Brazilian Pepper
(Schinus terebinthifolius)

It has been called Florida Holly, but it is not a holly. A native of Brazil, this tree has been widely planted. It has now spread deeply into wild areas and due to its very aggressive nature has crowded out much of the existing vegetation.

Birds, especially the migrating robins, love the berries of this tree. Brazilian Pepper seeds can still germinate after passing through a bird's digestive tract. So, by eating the berries, birds help disperse the seeds over a wide area.

Some people are sensitive to the sap and get a rash from trimming these trees. The sale or planting of Brazilian Pepper, Punk Trees, or Australian Pines is prohibited by law in Dade County because of the uncontrollable expansion of these species into areas where they are not desired.

Australian Pines *(Casuarina* spp.*)*

The name *Casuarina* is derived from the resemblance of the soft, fluffy "needles" to the feathers of the cassowary, a large ostrich-like bird which is common in the trees' native country of Australia.

The Australian Pine is a very controversial tree, loved by some as a graceful shade tree which provides shelter for picnickers along the beaches, and feared by others as a threat to native plant communities and a storm hazard. It is an aggressive tree which takes over areas and crowds out other species.

Nothing grows underneath an Australian Pine. It may just be the effects of shade, aggressive roots, and the heavy layer of needles, but some think that the needles release a chemical into the ground which eliminates competing plants. This theory is unproven.

The trees are a problem because their roots are shallow. They tend to blow over easily in storms and have been prohibited in some areas for this reason. The photo at top shows the shallow roots and the photo at left, the male flowers of a tree in full bloom.

There are three species of Australian Pine growing in Florida. *Casuarina equisetifolia* is common along the beaches. This tree is light-green in appearance with broad spreading branches. It has nitrogen-fixing root nodules which allow it to grow on sandy beach soils (see photo at right).

Casuarina equisetifolia has seed capsules visible most of the year. These capsules are, technically, not true cones and the Australian Pines are not true pines, but hardwoods. Sometimes called burrs, these seed capsules are rather sharp-pointed and not pleasant to walk over with bare feet. In the early part of the century when automobile tires were far more delicate than those of today, Australian Pine burrs were occasionally the cause of a flat tire (see photo, middle right).

Casuarina glauca is the second important species (see photo, bottom left). This tree does not form seeds, but reproduces by suckering. It is common to see many small trees arising from around its base. This tree has been planted along many of the drainage canals in the Miami area to stabilize the soil. In appearance, it is darker green and more vertical in shape than *Casuarina equisetifolia*.

Casuarina cunninghamiana is the third species. This species is more common in the central part of Florida because it is more cold resistant. It has been planted around tomato fields as a windbreak. It cannot tolerate the salt spray along the beaches.

This tree has no leaves in the usual sense of the word. The "needles" have many joints, each about one inch in length. Around each joint are tiny pointed structures which serve the functions of leaves. The surface of each segment of the "needles" can also produce food through photosynthesis.

A sure way to distinguish the various *Casuarina* species is to count the number of the tiny leaf structures around each "needle" segment. *Casuarina equisetifolia* generally has 7 and *Casuarina glauca* generally has 12 (see photo, middle left).

The trunks are sometimes pounded by woodpeckers, leaving rings of holes. These trees then look like they have been machine gun targets (see photo bottom right).

Australian Pines as "Eunuchs"

Some nurseries have grafted the top part of the suckering tree to the roots of the seeding tree to produce a tree which can neither seed nor sucker. The resulting tree cannot reproduce itself and does not create problems by spreading beyond the area where it is planted.

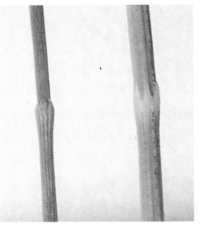

OAKS

Live Oak

Turkey Oak

Laurel Oak

Water Oak

Live Oak *(Quercus virginiana)*

This tree is called Live Oak because, although it sheds its leaves like the other oaks, it is never totally bare. It keeps at least a few green leaves at all times. Some of the Live Oaks in Florida are 300 years old.

Live Oak wood is extremely tough and was used for ship building. "Old Ironsides" was made of Live Oak and legend has it that its sides could repel cannonshot.

Oaks grow quite far north and the dropping of leaves in winter serves a useful purpose in the colder climates. Water lost through the leaves could not be replaced from frozen ground.

The flowering and growth of new leaves in the early spring makes a colorful display. The photo above shows the male flowers which appear on long tassles called "catkins."

The most common species of oaks in Florida can be identified by the shapes of their leaves. (Clockwise from top left: Live Oak *(Quercus virginiana)*; Turkey Oak *(Quercus laevis)*; Water Oak *(Quercus nigra)*; Laurel Oak *(Quercus laurifolia)*.

What's in an Oak Tree?

The air plants *(Tillandsia* spp.*)* in the photo above are epiphytes, that is, they grow on the tree but are not parasitic. They obtain their nourishment from rain water and debris that is washed down the tree trunk and from minerals leached from the tree leaves.

Spanish Moss *(Tillandsia usneoides)* is not a true moss (mosses have no flowers), but a bromeliad. Spanish Moss has tiny, yellow-green blooms which appear in the summer and are not generally noticed. It formerly had some value as furniture stuffing.

Spanish Moss is not a parasite, but simply uses the tree as a support. It can get thick enough to damage a tree, but does not kill trees as is commonly believed. Authors writing about the South frequently speak of the oaks being "festooned" with Spanish Moss. A related species is Ball Moss *(Tillandsia recurvata)* shown in the photo at upper left.

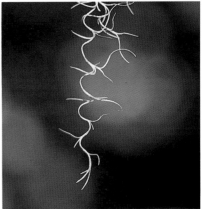

Mistletoe is visible in the bare oaks during winter

Mistletoe Berries

Squirrel's Nest

Galls

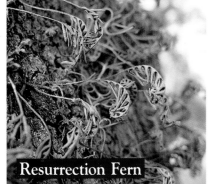

Resurrection Fern

After the rain

What's in an Oak? (continued)

Mistletoe is a parasite, unlike Spanish Moss. The white berries are poisonous to people, but are eaten by birds. A sticky substance on the seeds clings to the birds' beaks, and thus the seeds are transported to other trees.

Ancient Britons gathered European Mistletoe, a related species, at the winter solstice. Magical properties were attributed to the plant because its green leaves sprouted from naked trees in the middle of winter.

The bare branches of oak trees in winter reveal squirrel nests made of piled leaves along with the colonies of Mistletoe (photo above).

Oak Galls are abnormal growths caused by insects. The photos show four types. Although 400 different creatures can cause galls, most in Florida are caused by wasps depositing eggs under the bark of twigs. As the larvae grow, the tree forms galls around them.

The Resurrection Fern *(Polypodium polypodiodes)* appears dead when dry but bursts to life again after a rain. (bottom photos)

PINES

Slash Pine

Female Cones
Longleaf Pine

Longleaf Pine *(Pinus palustris)*
Slash Pine *(Pinus elliottii)*

The Longleaf and Slash Pines are the most common pines in south Florida. Longleaf Pine always has three or more needles per bundle, Slash Pine has either two or three. But, you can see the difference just by looking at the trees. The needles of Longleaf Pine are much longer and the shape of the needle clusters is different. The Slash Pine needles form a cylindrical shape around the end of each branch (see photo, above left) while the Longleaf Pine needles are arranged in a ball shape.

Pines do not produce flowers but instead, reproduce through male and female cones. In February, the male cones disperse pollen into the air in large quantities (below right). Cars, boats, mobile homes are all given a light dusting of the yellow substance. The tiny, newly formed female cones are shown in the photo, above, at right. These baby cones will enlarge to the more familiar size and shape shown on page 63 and will produce the seeds.

Male Cones
Longleaf Pine

Sand Pine

Sand Pine *(Pinus clausa)*

Sand Pines are less commonly seen in Florida. They prosper only in very dry soil, the kind of soil that would be bone dry only minutes after a heavy rain. This usually means a very sandy soil on a high ridge.

Cat-Faced Trees

Until the 1940's, the collection of sap for turpentine (or "marine stores," as the pine pitch was called) provided a living for many people. Diagonal slashes were cut into the trees' trunks in a "V" pattern and ceramic cups were hung from nails to catch the sap.

In the 1940's, a new process for making pulp into paper was introduced. This new process allowed the separation of the pitch by efficient chemical means so that collection by hand was no longer profitable.

There are many old pines in the midst of new housing subdivisions which bear the marks of turpentine collection. This photo shows one such tree with the metal guides for funneling the sap into the cup still attached to the trunk.

Candles of
Longleaf Pine

Candles of
Slash Pine

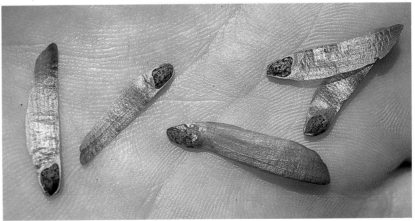

The new needles are formed on bud stems called "candles." When the trees "candle" each spring, it is another opportunity to easily distinguish the two main species. Slash Pine candles are long and thin (top right) and the candles of Longleaf Pine are shorter and thicker (photo, top left).

Pines are self-pruning at the lower part of the tree. As the tree grows taller, branches on the lower levels fall away. Knotholes form in the pine lumber in the places where the branches were attached to the tree trunk.

The photo at right shows that the cones of the Longleaf Pine are much larger than the Slash Pine cones. The chewed-up cones have been torn apart by squirrels who eat the seeds.

The seeds drop out as soon as the cones open. They have little wings which allow them to spiral and float on the breeze for considerable distances. The cones of some Sand Pines may remain on the tree and stay closed for years, opening only after the tree has been killed by fire.

The balmy warm climate of South Florida makes possible the cultivation of many beautiful exotic trees. Here are three of the many fantastic trees that could be grown here, but are not widely promoted by local nurseries.

Rose of Venezuela *(Brownea spp.)*

The spectacular blooms grow directly from the main stems of the tree. The ultra-long stamens contribute to the showy appearance.

Cannonball Tree *(Couroupita guianensis)*

This tree is grown for its novel flowers which are borne on special branches extending directly from the trunk of the tree. The Cannonball Tree produces a fruit which is about the size and weight of a bowling ball, but is unfortunately not edible. This tree is native to the Guianas.

Colville's Glory *(Colvillea racemosa)*

The photo of this tree is on page number one. Giant bunches of orange buds hang from this Madagascar native. Day by day, the buds open and reveal the orange-red blossoms.